THE WORLD OF NASCAR

MARK MARTIN: Perennial Contender

BY BRIAN C. PETERSON

T R A D I T I O N   B O O K S®
A New Tradition in Children's Publishing™
M A P L E   P L A I N ,   M I N N E S O T A

Published by **Tradition Books**® and distributed to the
school and library market by **The Child's World**®
P.O. Box 326
Chanhassen, MN 55317-0326
800/599-READ
http://www.childsworld.com

Photo Credits
Cover: Sports Gallery: Joe Robbins (bottom), Al Messerschmidt (top)
AP/Wide World: 9, 11, 15, 28
Corbis: 10, 13, 21
Dick Conway: 8, 14, 18, 19, 20, 23, 24
Sports Gallery: 5, 6, 26, 27 (Al Messerschmidt)

An Editorial Directions book
Editorial Directions, Inc.: E. Russell Primm, Editorial Director; Katie Marsico and Elizabeth K.
Martin, Assistant Editors; Olivia Nellums, Editorial Assistant; Susan Hindman, Copy Editor;
Susan Ashley, Proofreader; Kevin Cunningham, Fact Checker; Tim Griffin/IndexServ, Indexer;
James Buckley Jr., Photo Researcher and Selector

The Design Lab: Kathy Petelinsek, Art Director and Designer; Kari Thornborough,
Page Production

Library of Congress Cataloging-in-Publication Data
Peterson, Brian C.
  Mark Martin : perennial contender / by Brian C. Peterson.
    p. cm. — (The world of NASCAR)
Includes index.
Summary: A simple biography of racecar drive Mark Martin.
  ISBN 1-59187-031-3 (lib. bdg. : alk. paper)
  1. Martin, Mark, 1959– —Juvenile literature. 2. Automobile racing drivers—United States—
Biography—Juvenile literature. [1. Martin, Mark, 1959-- 2. Automobile racing drivers.]
I. Title. II. Series.
GV1032.M36 P48 2004
796.72'092—dc22   2003007689

Allen County Public Library

Note: Beginning with the 2004 season, the NASCAR
Winston Cup Series will be called the NASCAR Nextel
Cup Series.

M A R K   M A R T I N

Table of Contents

I N T R O D U C T I O N

Perennial Contender

Throughout Mark Martin's life, he has always had a need for speed. Whether he was riding his bicycle, running the bases, or driving in NASCAR, Martin wanted to be faster than anyone else.

He has certainly succeeded. Martin started out winning racing titles on dirt tracks. He became the all-time wins leader in the **NASCAR Busch Series.** And he has driven down Victory Lane 33 times during his NASCAR career.

He is one of the most complete racers in the modern era. Mark owns his own racing team, and has designed and built his own cars. He has also competed without large sponsorships. His attention to detail, hardworking attitude, and intense focus truly set him apart from other drivers.

The only thing Martin hasn't won is the NASCAR Winston

Cup Series championship. He's been close. During the past

15 years, it seemed as if the steely-eyed Martin was right on

the season leader's bumper.

Martin has earned the label of "Perennial Contender."

He has been called the best NASCAR driver ever who has

never won the Winston Cup, placing second four times

Five

(1990, '94, '98, and 2002). Since joining the Winston Cup

2009

Mark Martin's familiar No. 6 car roars through a turn.
Notice how the car is built very close to the ground to
help it hold speed through turns.

circuit in 1981, Martin has finished among the top 10 points leaders every year except 2001.

He has come so close to the top that he could taste it. But don't feel sad for the 43-year-old driver, who just finished his twentieth Winston Cup season.

"I don't care about [the attention], never cared about it," he said. "[It's] not important to me to be a superstar. It's important to me to be a winner."

"Mark Martin will retire a champion—with or without a [Winston Cup] title," said Martin's former crew chief and long-time friend Jimmy Fennig.

Here is the story of a man whose need for speed has kept him near the front of the pack for more than two decades.

Mark is one of the most popular drivers on the Winston Cup circuit, as well as one of the most successful.

CHAPTER ONE

Driving Was in His Blood

The thought of operating an 18-wheeled truck can intimidate most adults. Imagine driving down the interstate and seeing a 15-year-old on a booster seat at the controls of such a powerful vehicle. It wasn't uncommon for Mark Martin to take the wheel of his father's big rig. This was before he was even old enough to attend driver's education classes. Julian Martin, who owned a successful trucking firm in Batesville, Arkansas, was determined to be the only driving teacher his son needed.

Mark was born on January 9, 1959, in Batesville. He began learning the rules of the road at age five; by age 15, he was leasing his first 18-wheeler. Trucks, however, just didn't seem fast enough for Mark or Julian. Julian loved race cars, and Mark loved his father and racing, too.

"When Mark was ten, he and I built a fun car for ourselves to play with," Julian told Bob Zeller in a biography on Mark. "He had kinda long hair for then, just a little bitty chubby kid with long hair, and I would load my buddies up and say, 'Let's

Just getting started: Here's Mark with one of his first car transports. These big trucks often have the driver's name painted on the side.

have ol' Mark take us for a
ride.' We'd get in the back
seat, because it was more fun
to watch it from there. I had
taught him, 'When you shift
gears, you get it in gear or
you break the stick off. Don't
ever let me hear you get it in
partway.' So this 10-year-old
kid would get behind the
wheel, and he'd take off and
slam through the gears. And
every time he'd shift, his long
hair would jump off the back
of his head."

In 1973, Julian took Mark
to the superspeedways of
Daytona Beach, Florida, and

**The 14-year-old kid who went to Daytona with his
parents grew up to be a winner on the track many
times, including here in 2003 an IROC race.**

Talladega, Alabama. Mark was hooked on racing and told his
dad he wanted a car.

The next year, Julian and Mark modified a 1955 Chevy,
put a six-**cylinder** engine in it, and painted it red with
the No. 2 on the side. Mark was ready to roll at Locust
Grove—a .375-mile (.6-kilometer) dirt track about 7 miles
(11.26 km) southwest of Batesville that is now called the
Batesville Speedway.

Here's a closeup look at a 1955 Chevy, much like
the first car that young Mark raced with his friends
and family.

SPEED ON THE BASES

Mark Martin loved to drive race cars, but he also had other hobbies as a kid. He played Little League baseball and was especially good at stealing bases. In fact, he would leave notes on his father's desk signed "The Great Base Stealer."

Martin had his own kiln and enjoyed making ceramic pottery. He also kept tropical fish, eventually maintaining a 40-gallon (151.4-liter) tank.

A bicycle served as Martin's first set of wheels. That was followed by a **minibike,** which was always breaking down. Martin was never allowed to race motorcycles because his father, Julian, had been involved in a serious motorcycle accident.

Mark Martin on the basepaths? Nope, but when he was a kid, this was one of the things that the future NASCAR star was very good at.

C H A P T E R   T W O

Family Affair

In 1974, a teenaged Mark Martin and his father, Julian, formed the Bushes Brothers Race Team. The team was passionate about building a superior car, although its members did not have much experience doing it. They paid a lot of attention to detail, especially when it concerned the **roll cage** for protection.

Mark proved to be a natural, winning his second race at Locust Grove. On September 11, 1974, he captured the Arkansas State Championship at the Benton (Arkansas) Speedbowl.

"We ran really, really good," Martin told Zeller. "There were a lot of cars and a lot of **lapped traffic,** but I don't remember racing anybody. I won, and I don't know how to describe how big that win was. That wasn't weekly racing. It was a big event. There was a lot of competition on an unfamiliar track

under unfamiliar circumstances. It was one of the more out-
standing things I've done in my career."

Mark won 22 races, finished second 28 times, and third 36
times on the small local dirt tracks in 1974. In 1975, Mark won
51 of 96 races and finished second 32 times.

The Bushes Brothers Race Team decided to move up to
V-8 engines in 1976 and customized a Camaro, painting it
orange and white. Near the end of 1976, Julian and Mark took
their car to the half-mile asphalt track at Fairgrounds Speedway
in Springfield, Missouri.

Nose-to-tail at high speed, Mark and the Bushes
Brothers team raced Camaros like these in 1976.

Mark had never raced on asphalt before, but adapted quickly. It wasn't long before he and his dad were making the 200-mile (322-km) drive regularly to Springfield. Mark had developed a big following, mostly because of his age.

"I liked to slide the car," Martin told Zeller. "That was fun. Most of the tracks we ran were muddy racetracks, and we ran

Mark is in the red-and-white No. 31 car as he slides through a turn on an asphalt raceway in North Carolina.

pretty crossways in the corners. The dry, slick, black racetracks we tended to drive the cars straighter on. It was more like running on ice. But on a tacky, muddy racetrack, right before you got to the corners, you turned the steering wheel nearly backwards, and you mashed the gas wide open, and controlled the car with the throttle and steering wheel. A controlled slide was the fastest way around." The fastest way around was always the way that Mark Martin wanted to go.

This mud-track race from 1997 isn't that different from the mud-track races Mark starred in as he was coming up in the racing ranks.

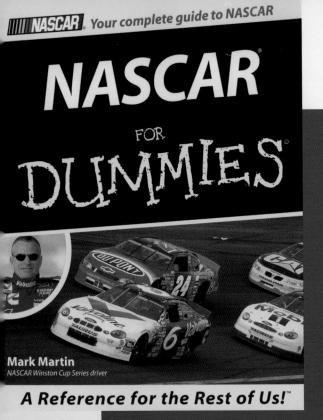

AUTHOR, AUTHOR

During his first two years of organized racing, Mark Martin kept a meticulous handwritten journal of his exploits. He recorded items such as where the race was held, the date, and a few notes about what took place. He also included what place he finished and how much money he won.

Some samples include:

"Heber Springs, April 13. Blew up second lap. No points."

"Locuse [he misspelled Locust] Grove, April 26. Not a good night. Too sticky for heavy car. 3 points. 33$."

In 1994, Martin had become an avid physical fitness buff. He coauthored *Strength Training for Performance Driving* with John S. Comereski.

"The future of motor sports depends on improvement in technology along with improvements in human performance. Improved performance can be attributed to strength training, proper dietary habits, stress control, and adequate rest," Martin wrote.

After sharing workout routines with racing fans, Martin turned to educating wannabe racing fans by writing *NASCAR for Dummies* in 2000.

"I decided the best way to explain my love for NASCAR racing wasn't by sticking fans in a race car and making them drive laps around Daytona," he wrote. "It was by writing this book. If you can't discover the beauty of this sport by doing—and riding down the highway going 80 mph in your Honda Accord doesn't count—you may as well discover it by reading."

From racer to author: This is the book Mark co-wrote in 2000, giving racing fans an insider's look at NASCAR racing.

C H A P T E R   T H R E E

Rising Star

Mark Martin was making local headlines by 1976 and had earned the nickname "The Kid." He had become so popular that he won the Driver of the Year contest in *Victory Lane,* a weekly racing newspaper in Springfield, Missouri.

The Kid didn't waste any time keeping up with the big boys when he renamed his racing team The Mark Martin Racing Team. His team joined the American Speed Association (ASA) short-track stock car series in 1977. The ASA was the premier Midwestern short-track series, and Martin earned rookie-of-the-year honors while still a senior in high school.

At age 19 in 1978, Martin became the youngest ASA champion ever. He also was offered an opportunity to drive in the Daytona 500, which he turned down—probably because he was

too busy. A typical week for Martin included Springfield on Friday, Janesville (Wisconsin) on Saturday, Michigan on Sunday morning, and Toledo, Ohio, on Sunday night. The rest of the week was for fine-tuning the car.

Martin won three ASA titles in a row (1978–1980). With Ray Dillon, he helped revolutionize the short-track series by designing and producing a lighter super **chassis,** the Mark II. It didn't take long before every competitor was using the Mark II.

Despite his success, Martin still questioned whether he would ever fulfill his dream of driving on the NASCAR circuit. "That's when I began to wonder if I'd ever make it," Martin

Just old enough to drive, here's Mark with his ASA race car in 1978, on his way to the series championship.

said in 1979. "It's really tough and it costs so much to run there. I can't do it now because of the cost. I've talked to a few companies about sponsoring me, but they aren't interested in advertising with a race car. I used to have [long-range] goals, but most of them have mellowed out. There's no way of getting into NASCAR on less than a quarter of a million dollars. I've seen drivers try and come back, not because they couldn't drive, but because they couldn't afford it."

On a shoestring budget, Martin's dream became reality in 1981 when he ran his own cars in NASCAR on a limited basis. All he wanted from his first season was to win a **pole position** or earn a victory.

By 1982, Mark had moved up to Winston Cup, sponsored at first by Apache Stove, as shown by his hat.

Martin made his Winston Cup debut on April 3, 1981, at North Wilkesboro Speedway (North Carolina), but had to drop out after 166 laps. He won the pole in his third race at Nashville and proceeded to win another pole at Richmond, Virginia. He posted his first top-five finish at Martinsville.

It seemed that the stars were aligning for Martin. All the things he was known for—hard work, commitment to his craft, knowledge of the cars, and attention to detail—had him on the fast track for stardom.

Before he got his familiar No. 6 car, Mark ran with No. 02. Above, he is "getting loose" on a turn at a 1983 race.

STOCK CAR'S "MINOR LEAGUES"

While driving on the American Speed Association (ASA) short-track stock car series, Mark Martin raced against other future NASCAR stars such as Rusty Wallace, Darrell Waltrip, Donnie Allison, and Dick Trickle.

Series such as ASA are important proving grounds for NASCAR drivers. They can also get experience in United States Auto Club racing, as 2002 NASCAR champion Tony Stewart did. Off-road racing is another way to learn to race. Hot young driver Jimmie Johnson spent time bouncing pickup trucks over desert courses before he joined "the big leagues."

When drivers earn a spot in the Busch Series, they are one step away from stardom in NASCAR's highest level, the Winston Cup.

Who needs a road? Taking part in off-road races through deserts and wasteland is one way that drivers earn a NASCAR ride.

C H A P T E R   F O U R

The Comeback Kid

I n 1982, Mark Martin moved to North Carolina and built his own car. Apache Stove, a small manufacturer of wood- and coal-burning stoves in North Carolina, signed on as his main sponsor for $50,000. Other teams were getting as much as $400,000 from their top sponsors.

But those were the only things that seemed to go right for Martin that year, and the bottom proceeded to fall out of his racing career. He struggled to finish races and soon ran out of money, especially when Apache Stove took back its offer. In April 1983, Martin was forced to sell his entire operation.

The next season was even worse. Martin raced poorly for three different teams. He became so depressed that he began drinking alcohol to forget his troubles.

One thing did go right for Martin at Christmas in 1983.

His sister Glenda introduced him to Arlene Everett. Martin

returned to racing in the ASA and asked Arlene to marry him

in 1984. In 1986, he won his fourth ASA title.

Things began to change for the better in 1987. Martin

agreed to drive a Ford in the NASCAR Busch Series, which is

one step below the Winston Cup. He moved his family back to

North Carolina and won three races. The Busch Series proved to

be a great move for him. He won a record 45 races in the series.

Mark proudly holds up a trophy he won at a Busch
Series race in North Carolina in 1987. Mark has won
more Busch races than any other driver.

Martin's big break finally came when Jack Roush, a former

Ford engineer who had become a multimillionaire, hired Martin

to drive for him in 1988. After struggling in his first year, Martin

won his first NASCAR event, defeating Rusty Wallace at

Rockingham, North Carolina, in 1989. In 1990, Martin won

No. 6 was No. 2: Here's Mark battling in a 1990 race.
By the end of the season, he had finished second in
the Winston Cup standings.

three times and went on to finish second to Dale Earnhardt Sr. in the Winston Cup standings.

Martin credited Roush with making a difference in his career. "Jack identifies with people who want it really bad and are willing to work really, really hard and really deserve an opportunity," Martin said. "And those are the types of people that Jack likes. He likes to give people a chance to realize their dreams. And he is indescribably loyal to people who have the right heart and desire and work ethic.

"He's been a solid figure in my life. We're cut from the same cloth. Our desire to win and our motivation are a lot alike. We've been through a lot together, and we've stayed shoulder to shoulder."

During the past 15 years with Roush, Martin has won more than $30 million in prize money and has recorded more victories than all but 16 other drivers in NASCAR history. In 1998, he became the only driver to win four International Race of Champions (IROC) titles. IROC races

pit top drivers from different types of motor sports racing in identical cars.

However, after so much success in the 1990s, Martin had arguably the worst season of his NASCAR career in 2001, with just three top-five finishes and finishing twelfth in the points standings. "I was under tremendous stress and pressure to try to revive my career," Martin told *Sporting News.* "I felt like I was losing my career. I'm not going to race for 20th or 25th place."

Martin made another great comeback in 2002. Just when everybody thought his great career might be at its end, he post-

Mark's 1997 car is reflected in a puddle of rainwater before a 1997 race at Talladega.

ed 12 top-five finishes.. He finished the season only 38 points behind winner Tony Stewart in the Winston Cup standings.

"We gave it everything we had," Martin said. "What an effort. My only regret is that I could have provided more leadership to where we could have scored another hundred to hundred and fifty points to win the title hands down. I did all I could, and I'm proud of what we accomplished."

Martin has done a lot to be proud of. With his fast finish in 2002, he's sure to keep adding to his list of accomplishments in the years ahead.

Still ready to race, Mark Martin expects to find himself in the driver's seat for years to come.

THE NEXT GENERATION

Only seven years after Matt Martin, Mark's only son, was born in 1991, he was racing **quarter-midget cars** in Florida. It didn't take long for Matt to become a success.

In fact, Mark organized a local group in Daytona Beach, Florida, to build a quarter-midget oval so that he could see Matt race more often. Matt has become a celebrity in his own right. He appeared with Mark on boxes of Life and Cap'n Crunch cereals. He even has his own Web site, *www.mattmartin.net.* In 2002, 10-year-old Matt also planned on moving up to the next step and racing **Bandoleros.**

"That [having Matt become a racer in the future] is not important to he or I right now," says Mark Martin. "We're having fun. We won a lot of races in 2002, which has been more fun. You learn life experiences by racing these cars, stuff you can use every day in life. The disappointment or the thrill, excitement or gratification, or incredible hardship or unfair circumstances—those things are part of life you have to deal with, no matter if you race or not."

Mark's son, Matt, has become a top quarter-midget racer. Above, dad gives his son a few pointers before a race.

MARK MARTIN'S LIFE

1959   Born on January 9 in Batesville, Arkansas

1974   On April 12, officially begins his racing career in six-cylinder stock class at Locust Grove Racetrack near Batesville

1977   Joins the American Speed Association (ASA) short-track stock car series and wins rookie-of-the-year honors

1978   Becomes youngest (19) champion in ASA history and proceeds to win three consecutive titles (1978–1980)

1981   Makes NASCAR Winston Cup Series debut at North Wilkesboro Speedway

1986   Wins fourth ASA championship

1987   Makes NASCAR Busch Series debut and wins three races

1989   Wins his first NASCAR Winston Cup Series race at Rockingham (North Carolina) on October 22

1990   Wins three races and finishes second to Dale Earnhardt Sr. in Winston Cup points standings

1993   Becomes sixth driver in modern era of Winston Cup to win four consecutive races

1994   Finishes second in Winston Cup points standings

1997   Sets the all-time record on NASCAR Busch Series with 32nd victory

1998   Sets a single-season career-high with seven victories and finishes second in Winston Cup points standings

2002   Finishes second in Winston Cup points standings

GLOSSARY

Bandolero—an odd little toad-shaped car that weighs approximately 550 pounds (250 kilograms) and is powered by a 30-horsepower, 570cc engine; it can go as fast as 70 miles (112.6 km) per hour

chassis—the steel frame of a car

cylinders—the tubes in an engine block in which the pistons move up and down; the number of cylinders and their configuration determine the engine type (V-6 or V-8).

lapped traffic—cars that are a lap or more behind the leaders, but can still get in the way of front-running racers

minibike—a small one-passenger motorcycle with a low frame and raised handlebars

NASCAR Busch Series—a steppingstone to NASCAR's Winston Cup Series, which began in 1982; Busch races usually are held on Saturdays in conjunction with Winston Cup races

pole position—the fastest driver in qualifying trials starts the race at this best position, which is the inside spot on the front row

quarter-midget car—a 6-foot (1.8 meter), open-wheeled race car with a single-cylinder engine and full suspension

roll cage—the protective frame of steel surrounding a driver; the roll cage consists of roll bars, which are made from steel tubing

FOR MORE INFORMATION ABOUT MARK MARTIN

Books

Comereski, John S, and Mark Martin. *Strength Training for Performance Driving.* Osceola, Wis.: Motorbooks International Publishers & Wholesalers, 1994.

Martin, Mark. *NASCAR for Dummies.* New York: Wiley Publishing, Inc., 2000.

Zeller, Bob, with foreword by Mark Martin. *Mark Martin: Driven to Race.* Phoenix: David Bull Publishing, 1997.

Web Sites

ESPN

http://rpm.espn.go.com/rpm/index
For complete coverage of all NASCAR events from one of the nation's leading sports information providers

The Official Web Site of NASCAR

http://www.nascar.com
For an overview of each season of NASCAR, as well as the history of the sport, statistics, and a dictionary of racing terms

The Official Web Site of Roush Racing

http://www.roushracing.com
For loads of information on all of the Roush Racing drivers, including Mark Martin

INDEX

ABOUT THE AUTHOR

Brian C. Peterson has been a professional sportswriter for more than a decade, covering pro football, the Olympics, and other sports. He has written two books, *Terrell Davis* and *NFL Rules!*, and his articles have appeared in publications such as the *New York Times, Boston Globe, NFL Insider,* and *NFL GameDay.* Peterson resides with his wife and two young children in Torrance, California.